★ THE ★
UNITED
STATES
PRESIDENTS

MILLARD
FILLMORE

Heidi M.D. Elston

Checkerboard
Library

An Imprint of Abdo Publishing
abdobooks.com

ABDOBOOKS.COM

Published by Abdo Publishing, a division of ABDO, PO Box 398166, Minneapolis, Minnesota 55439. Copyright © 2021 by Abdo Consulting Group, Inc. International copyrights reserved in all countries. No part of this book may be reproduced in any form without written permission from the publisher. Checkerboard Library™ is a trademark and logo of Abdo Publishing.

Printed in the United States of America, North Mankato, Minnesota
052020
092020

THIS BOOK CONTAINS
RECYCLED MATERIALS

Design: Emily O'Malley, Kelly Doudna, Mighty Media, Inc.
Production: Mighty Media, Inc.
Editor: Jessica Rusick

Cover Photograph: Alamy
Interior Photographs: Albert de Bruijn/iStockphoto, p. 37; AP Images, p. 36; Classic Image/Alamy, pp. 16, 21; Getty Images, p. 14; Hulton Archive/Getty Images, p. 11; Library of Congress, pp. 5, 6, 7, 17, 18, 20, 27, 29, 40; Mathew Brady/Getty Images, p. 28; North Wind Picture Archives, p. 23; North Wind Picture Archives/Alamy, pp. 12, 31; Pete Souza/Flickr, p. 44; Philip Scalia/Alamy, p. 13; Pictorial Press Ltd/Alamy, p. 19; Shutterstock Images, pp. 38, 39; Stock Montage/Getty Images, p. 15; Vespasian/Alamy, p. 33; Wikimedia Commons, pp. 7 (Caroline Fillmore), 25, 32, 40 (Washington), 42

Library of Congress Control Number: 2019956443

Publisher's Cataloging-in-Publication Data
Names: Elston, Heidi M.D., author.
Title: Millard Fillmore / by Heidi M.D. Elston
Description: Minneapolis, Minnesota : Abdo Publishing, 2021 | Series: The United States presidents | Includes online resources and index.
Identifiers: ISBN 9781532193484 (lib. bdg.) | ISBN 9781098212124 (ebook)
Subjects: LCSH: Fillmore, Millard, 1800-1874--Juvenile literature. | Presidents--Biography--Juvenile literature. | Presidents--United States--History--Juvenile literature. | Legislators--United States—Biography--Juvenile literature. | Politics and government--Biography--Juvenile literature.
Classification: DDC 973.64092--dc23

★ CONTENTS ★

Millard Fillmore

Millard Fillmore was the thirteenth president of the United States. He led the country during one of the worst times in American history. The North and the South argued about slavery. Later, these arguments led to the American **Civil War**.

In 1828, Fillmore began working in politics. Four years later, he won election to the US House of Representatives.

In 1848, Zachary Taylor was elected president. Fillmore served as his vice president. Just 16 months after taking office, President Taylor died. Fillmore then became president.

As president, Fillmore helped pass the Compromise of 1850. He thought the compromise would solve the country's slavery problems. But neither the North nor the South was satisfied with the new laws. President Fillmore was so unpopular that he did not run for reelection.

Fillmore did what he thought was right for the country. He loved the United States and wanted to avoid war. He actively served his community and country throughout his life.

★ TIMELINE ★

1800
On January 7, Millard Fillmore was born in Cayuga County, New York.

1823
Fillmore began practicing law in East Aurora, New York.

1826
On February 5, Fillmore married Abigail Powers.

1832
Fillmore won election to the US House of Representatives.

1834
Fillmore joined the Whig Party.

1844
Fillmore ran for governor of New York but lost the election.

1847
Fillmore was elected the comptroller of New York State.

1849
On March 5, Fillmore became vice president under Zachary Taylor.

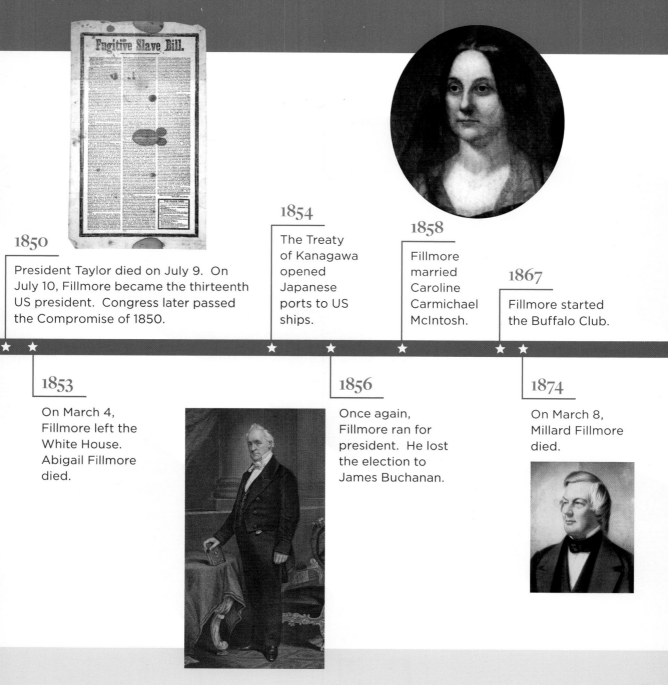

1850
President Taylor died on July 9. On July 10, Fillmore became the thirteenth US president. Congress later passed the Compromise of 1850.

1854
The Treaty of Kanagawa opened Japanese ports to US ships.

1858
Fillmore married Caroline Carmichael McIntosh.

1867
Fillmore started the Buffalo Club.

1853
On March 4, Fillmore left the White House. Abigail Fillmore died.

1856
Once again, Fillmore ran for president. He lost the election to James Buchanan.

1874
On March 8, Millard Fillmore died.

"An honorable defeat is better than a dishonorable victory.**"**

MILLARD FILLMORE

DID YOU KNOW?

★ Millard Fillmore was the first president to have a stepmother.

★ In 1855, Oxford University in Oxford, England, offered Fillmore an honorary degree. He refused it. The degree was written in Latin, which Fillmore couldn't read.

★ In 1819, Fillmore bought the first book he had ever owned. It was a dictionary.

★ Abigail Fillmore was the first First Lady to hold a job after getting married.

★ Abigail Fillmore started the White House library.

Young Millard

Millard Fillmore was born in a log cabin in Cayuga County, New York, on January 7, 1800. He was the second child born to Nathaniel and Phoebe Fillmore. Millard had three sisters and five brothers.

As a boy, Millard worked on the family farm. Because he worked so much, he went to school only three months each year. Still, he learned reading, writing, arithmetic, and geography.

When Millard was 14, he became an **apprentice** wool worker. He agreed to work for seven years. However, after five years, Millard left the job. He paid his employer $30 to free him from the agreement.

At 19, Millard moved to Buffalo, New York. He found a job in a law office. Millard had not spent much time in school. But he was smart and loved to read. He got another part-time job teaching school.

FAST FACTS

BORN: January 7, 1800

WIVES: Abigail Powers (1798–1853), Caroline Carmichael McIntosh (1813–1881)

CHILDREN: 2

POLITICAL PARTY: Whig

AGE AT INAUGURATION: 50

YEARS SERVED: 1850–1853

VICE PRESIDENT: none

DIED: March 8, 1874, age 74

Millard's boyhood home

Millard studied law under a local judge. In 1823, he became a lawyer. For seven years, Millard practiced law in East Aurora, New York. Then, he moved his law firm to Buffalo. There, his business grew. Millard's law practice soon became one of the best known in the state!

Family Man and Congressman

On February 5, 1826, Fillmore married Abigail Powers. Abigail had been born in Stillwater, New York, in 1798.

Abigail Fillmore

She was well educated and loved to read. From the time she was 16 years old, Abigail had taught school.

To bring in extra money, Abigail continued teaching until 1828. The Fillmores then raised two children. Millard Powers was born later that year. Mary Abigail followed in 1832.

Also in 1828, Fillmore began working in politics. That year, he was elected to the New York state legislature. At that time, people who couldn't pay

The Fillmores lived in this East Aurora home from 1826 to 1830.

their **debts** were commonly put in prison. Fillmore worked to pass laws forbidding this punishment for debt. Citizens of New York were happy with him.

In 1832, Fillmore won election to the US House of Representatives. He served in Congress from 1833 to 1835 and from 1837 to 1843. In 1834, Fillmore joined the **Whig** Party.

Fillmore (*pictured*) became a representative while Andrew Jackson was president. Fillmore supported the Whig Party's strong opposition to the president.

Fillmore served as chairman of the House Ways and Means Committee. As chairman, he helped make laws that taxed goods from other countries. These high taxes increased demand for American-made goods. This helped US businesses, and the US **economy** improved. As a result, Fillmore and the **Whig** Party grew popular.

As a congressman, Fillmore supported new inventions and businesses. He helped provide inventor Samuel F.B. Morse with $30,000 to help develop the **telegraph**. This invention helped Americans communicate over long distances.

Samuel Morse sent the first message over his telegraph in May 1844. It read, "What hath God wrought?"

New Nominations

Lewis Cass

Fillmore ran for governor of New York in 1844. He lost the election. Fillmore then returned to his law practice. But he did not give up on politics. In 1847, Fillmore was elected the state comptroller. In this position, he handled New York's money.

In 1848, the **Whig** Party chose Zachary Taylor to run for president. Fillmore was named his **running mate**. The **Democrats** nominated Senator Lewis Cass for president. William Butler was chosen as Cass's running mate.

During the campaign, slavery was an important issue. Taylor was a Southerner who owned slaves. Fillmore was an antislavery Northerner. Together, they appealed to many Americans.

Cass believed that the people in a territory should decide whether slavery should be allowed there. Because of Cass's views, his nomination angered many **Democrats**. Those members then split from the party. They voted for **Free-Soil** candidate Martin Van Buren. The split helped Taylor and Fillmore win the election. They won 163 electoral votes to Cass's 127!

Martin Van Buren

Vice President Fillmore

President Taylor

Fillmore and Taylor did not meet until after the 1848 election. The two men came from very different backgrounds. They found they did not agree on many issues.

On March 5, 1849, Fillmore began his duties as vice president. His main duty was to govern the US Senate.

At that time, many senators were caught up in bitter arguments over issues such as slavery. Fillmore insisted that the senators respect each other.

He helped bring order to the Senate.

In 1850, the Senate began **debating** a set of resolutions. Kentucky senator Henry Clay proposed them. Clay hoped his resolutions would end the slavery arguments. They became known as the Compromise of 1850.

President Taylor was against the compromise. He would not pass it. Then, everything changed. Zachary Taylor died on July 9, 1850. By law, Vice President Fillmore became president.

As vice president, Fillmore felt shut out of President Taylor's administration.

Compromise of 1850

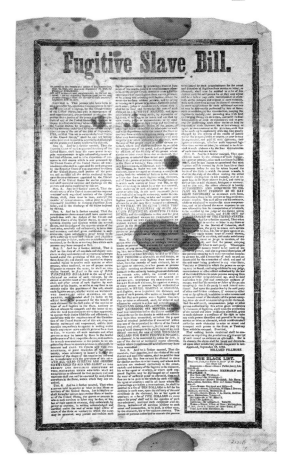

Fillmore signed the Fugitive Slave Act into law in September 1850. He did not like the law. But he knew it followed the US Constitution.

Fillmore took the oath of office on July 10. He got right to work. President Fillmore supported the Compromise of 1850. So, he replaced Taylor's **cabinet** with men who also supported the compromise.

The compromise said that California should be admitted as a free state. It banned slave trading in Washington, DC. And, it said the New Mexico and Utah Territories could allow slavery if they wanted to.

The compromise included the Fugitive Slave Act. This act stated that runaway slaves could be captured and returned to their masters. Anyone who hid runaway slaves would be punished. The Fugitive Slave Act angered those against slavery.

President Fillmore believed that without these new laws, a **civil war** would start. Then, the United States would break apart. Fillmore wanted to settle the slavery problem while preserving unity. In September, Congress passed the Compromise of 1850. President Fillmore was sure the slavery problem was solved.

SUPREME COURT APPOINTMENT

BENJAMIN R. CURTIS: 1851

Many people hoped Henry Clay's Compromise of 1850 would be the final solution to the slavery issue. Instead, it just delayed civil war for ten years.

The Thirteenth President

President Fillmore also worked to establish trading rights with other countries. He sent Commodore Matthew C. Perry on an expedition to Japan. This led to the Treaty of Kanagawa in 1854. This treaty opened Japanese ports to US ships. The United States profited from Japan. President Fillmore also lowered the US postal rate from five to three cents.

While president, Fillmore spent most of his time dealing with the slavery issue. The Compromise of 1850 was not working. Americans still fought over slavery.

The Fugitive Slave Act was the biggest problem. President Fillmore found it difficult to enforce the act. Often, antislavery Northerners felt the president was siding with proslavery Southerners. Some Northern states even passed laws preventing the act's enforcement.

Several incidents tested President Fillmore's ability to enforce the Fugitive Slave Act. One incident occurred in 1851. Maryland slave owner Edward Gorsuch traveled to

Commodore Matthew C. Perry

Pennsylvania, a free state. Four of his slaves had escaped to Christiana, Pennsylvania. On September 11, a gunfight broke out. The slaves and local citizens fought Gorsuch, who died.

Afterward, more than 40 people were charged with treason. Northerners were angry. They felt the slaves were only defending themselves.

This incident led to the largest treason trial in US history. The defendants were declared innocent. The judge ruled that opposing the Fugitive Slave Act did not amount to treason. This ruling angered many Southerners. President Fillmore was caught between the North and the South. Neither side was happy with him.

Also that year, 2,000 people broke into a jail in Syracuse, New York. They freed a runaway slave. President Fillmore's attempts to punish anyone failed. The president's popularity continued to fall.

Fillmore believed the Compromise of 1850 would keep the United States together. Instead, it was pulling the country apart. By 1861, 11 states would leave the United States and form their own country.

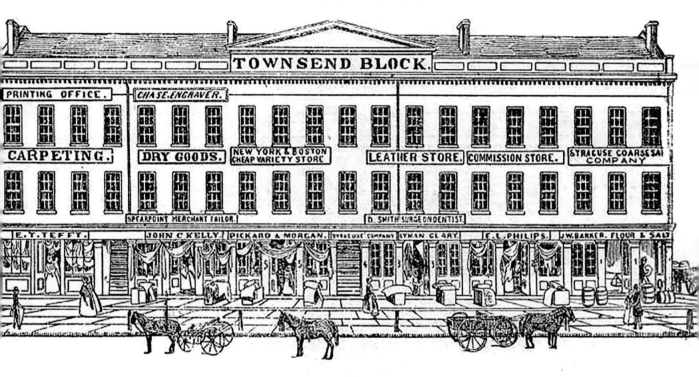

The runaway slave in Syracuse was named Jerry. The Townsend building in downtown Syracuse was renamed the Jerry Rescue Building to commemorate his escape from jail.

PRESIDENT FILLMORE'S CABINET

ONE TERM
July 10, 1850–March 4, 1853

- ★ **STATE:** Daniel Webster
  Edward Everett (from November 6, 1852)

- ★ **TREASURY:** Thomas Corwin

- ★ **WAR:** George Washington Crawford
  Charles Magill Conrad (from August 15, 1850)

- ★ **NAVY:** William Alexander Graham
  John P. Kennedy (from July 26, 1852)

- ★ **ATTORNEY GENERAL:** Reverdy Johnson
  John J. Crittenden (from August 14, 1850)

- ★ **INTERIOR:** Thomas Ewing
  T.M.T. McKennan (from August 15, 1850)
  Alexander H.H. Stuart (from September 16, 1850)

President Millard Fillmore

After the White House

The **Whig** Party did not nominate Fillmore to run for president in 1852. Fillmore knew he would not be chosen. Signing the Compromise of 1850 had angered antislavery Whigs.

Instead, the Whigs chose General Winfield Scott to run for president. Scott was against slavery. The Whigs hoped Scott would unite the party and win the election. But the Whigs lost the election to **Democrat** Franklin Pierce. As a political party, the Whigs were almost finished. Fillmore was the last Whig president in US history.

General Winfield Scott

On March 4, 1853, Fillmore left the White House. He returned to Buffalo and his law practice. Just 26 days later, Abigail Fillmore died of **pneumonia**. Fillmore was greatly saddened by the death of his wife. One year later, tragedy struck again. His daughter, Mary, died suddenly. Fillmore was heartbroken. To keep busy, he returned to politics.

Franklin Pierce served as president from 1853 to 1857.

Know-Nothings

The United States and its politics were changing. Between the mid-1840s and the mid-1850s, nearly 3 million people **immigrated** to the United States. Germans moved to the Midwest, and Irish arrived in the East. Many native-born Americans felt threatened by this wave of immigrants.

In response, a secret group formed in the 1840s. Its members wanted to pass laws against these newcomers. The people in this group called themselves the Know-Nothings. Soon, the Know-Nothings organized a new political party. They called it the American Party.

The American Party wanted limitations placed on immigration and immigrants. Its members felt that immigrants should be barred from voting or holding public office. And, they wanted to impose a requirement on citizenship. Anyone seeking citizenship would first need to live in the country for 21 years.

The American Party gained power during the 1850s. It won many seats in Congress. But the party's popularity did not last long. It fell apart after 1856.

Fillmore did not agree with the American Party's anti-immigrant message.

Return to Buffalo

Fillmore decided to run for president again in 1856. The **Whig** Party and the American Party joined together. Fillmore was their presidential candidate. John C. Frémont was the **Republican** Party candidate. The **Democrats** nominated James Buchanan.

Caroline Fillmore

In November, Fillmore lost the election to Buchanan. After this loss, Fillmore moved to Buffalo. He left politics for good. But he continued to support other politicians.

In 1858, Fillmore married Caroline Carmichael McIntosh. The couple had many friends they enjoyed spending time with. In Buffalo, Fillmore did much for his city. He supported the city's libraries. Fillmore also represented the Buffalo Board of Trade. He became the first **chancellor** of the University of Buffalo. And, he helped start the Buffalo General Hospital.

Fillmore founded and served as the first president of the Buffalo Historical Society. In 1867, he helped start a social club called the Buffalo Club. As the club's first president, Fillmore greeted many important visitors to the city.

Fillmore spent his last years close to his wife, who was ill. On March 8, 1874, Millard Fillmore died after suffering two **strokes**.

While Fillmore was president, slavery had divided the nation. He tried his best to solve this problem with wisdom and laws. Millard Fillmore worked hard to preserve the United States.

Outside Buffalo's city hall stands a statue in Fillmore's honor.

BRANCHES OF GOVERNMENT

The US government is divided into three branches. They are the executive, legislative, and judicial branches. This division is called a separation of powers. Each branch has some power over the others. This is called a system of checks and balances.

★ EXECUTIVE BRANCH

The executive branch enforces laws. It is made up of the president, the vice president, and the president's cabinet. The president represents the United States around the world. He or she oversees relations with other countries and signs treaties. The president signs bills into law and appoints officials and federal judges. He or she also leads the military and manages government workers.

★ LEGISLATIVE BRANCH

The legislative branch makes laws, maintains the military, and regulates trade. It also has the power to declare war. This branch consists of the Senate and the House of Representatives. Together, these two houses make up Congress. Each state has two senators. A state's population determines the number of representatives it has.

★ JUDICIAL BRANCH

The judicial branch interprets laws. It consists of district courts, courts of appeals, and the Supreme Court. District courts try cases. If a person disagrees with a trial's outcome, he or she may appeal. If a court of appeals supports the ruling, a person may appeal to the Supreme Court. The Supreme Court also makes sure that laws follow the US Constitution.

THE PRESIDENT ★

★ QUALIFICATIONS FOR OFFICE

To be president, a person must meet three requirements. A candidate must be at least 35 years old and a natural-born US citizen. He or she must also have lived in the United States for at least 14 years.

★ ELECTORAL COLLEGE

The US presidential election is an indirect election. Voters from each state choose electors to represent them in the Electoral College. The number of electors from each state is based on the state's population. Each elector has one electoral vote. Electors are pledged to cast their vote for the candidate who receives the highest number of popular votes in their state. A candidate must receive the majority of Electoral College votes to win.

★ TERM OF OFFICE

Each president may be elected to two four-year terms. Sometimes, a president may only be elected once. This happens if he or she served more than two years of the previous president's term.

The presidential election is held on the Tuesday after the first Monday in November. The president is sworn in on January 20 of the following year. At that time, he or she takes the oath of office:

> *I do solemnly swear (or affirm) that I will faithfully execute the office of President of the United States, and will to the best of my ability, preserve, protect and defend the Constitution of the United States.*

LINE OF SUCCESSION ★

The Presidential Succession Act of 1947 defines who becomes president if the president cannot serve. The vice president is first in the line of succession. Next are the Speaker of the House and the President Pro Tempore of the Senate. If none of these individuals is able to serve, the office falls to the president's cabinet members. They would take office in the order in which each department was created:

Secretary of State

Secretary of the Treasury

Secretary of Defense

Attorney General

Secretary of the Interior

Secretary of Agriculture

Secretary of Commerce

Secretary of Labor

Secretary of Health and Human Services

Secretary of Housing and Urban Development

Secretary of Transportation

Secretary of Energy

Secretary of Education

Secretary of Veterans Affairs

Secretary of Homeland Security

While in office, the president receives a salary of $400,000 each year. He or she lives in the White House and has 24-hour Secret Service protection.

The president may travel on a Boeing 747 jet called Air Force One. The airplane can accommodate 76 passengers. It has kitchens, a dining room, sleeping areas, and a conference room. It also has fully equipped offices with the latest communications systems. Air Force One can fly halfway around the world before needing to refuel. It can even refuel in flight!

Air Force One

If the president wishes to travel by car, he or she uses Cadillac One. It has been modified with heavy armor and communications systems. The president takes

Cadillac One

Cadillac One along when visiting other countries if secure transportation will be needed.

The president also travels on a helicopter called Marine One. Like the presidential car, Marine One accompanies the president when traveling abroad if necessary.

Sometimes, the president needs to get away and relax with family and friends. Camp David is the official presidential retreat. It is located in the cool, wooded mountains of Maryland. The US Navy maintains the retreat, and the US Marine Corps keeps it secure. The camp offers swimming, tennis, golf, and hiking.

When the president leaves office, he or she receives lifetime Secret Service protection. He or she also receives a yearly pension of $207,800 and funding for office space, supplies, and staff.

Marine One

George Washington

Abraham Lincoln

Theodore Roosevelt

	PRESIDENT	PARTY	TOOK OFFICE
1	George Washington	None	April 30, 1789
2	John Adams	Federalist	March 4, 1797
3	Thomas Jefferson	Democratic-Republican	March 4, 1801
4	James Madison	Democratic-Republican	March 4, 1809
5	James Monroe	Democratic-Republican	March 4, 1817
6	John Quincy Adams	Democratic-Republican	March 4, 1825
7	Andrew Jackson	Democrat	March 4, 1829
8	Martin Van Buren	Democrat	March 4, 1837
9	William H. Harrison	Whig	March 4, 1841
10	John Tyler	Whig	April 6, 1841
11	James K. Polk	Democrat	March 4, 1845
12	Zachary Taylor	Whig	March 5, 1849
13	Millard Fillmore	Whig	July 10, 1850
14	Franklin Pierce	Democrat	March 4, 1853
15	James Buchanan	Democrat	March 4, 1857
16	Abraham Lincoln	Republican	March 4, 1861
17	Andrew Johnson	Democrat	April 15, 1865
18	Ulysses S. Grant	Republican	March 4, 1869
19	Rutherford B. Hayes	Republican	March 3, 1877

LEFT OFFICE	TERMS SERVED	VICE PRESIDENT
March 4, 1797	Two	John Adams
March 4, 1801	One	Thomas Jefferson
March 4, 1809	Two	Aaron Burr, George Clinton
March 4, 1817	Two	George Clinton, Elbridge Gerry
March 4, 1825	Two	Daniel D. Tompkins
March 4, 1829	One	John C. Calhoun
March 4, 1837	Two	John C. Calhoun, Martin Van Buren
March 4, 1841	One	Richard M. Johnson
April 4, 1841	Died During First Term	John Tyler
March 4, 1845	Completed Harrison's Term	Office Vacant
March 4, 1849	One	George M. Dallas
July 9, 1850	Died During First Term	Millard Fillmore
March 4, 1853	Completed Taylor's Term	Office Vacant
March 4, 1857	One	William R.D. King
March 4, 1861	One	John C. Breckinridge
April 15, 1865	Served One Term, Died During Second Term	Hannibal Hamlin, Andrew Johnson
March 4, 1869	Completed Lincoln's Second Term	Office Vacant
March 4, 1877	Two	Schuyler Colfax, Henry Wilson
March 4, 1881	One	William A. Wheeler

Franklin D. Roosevelt

John F. Kennedy

Ronald Reagan

	PRESIDENT	PARTY	TOOK OFFICE
20	James A. Garfield	Republican	March 4, 1881
21	Chester Arthur	Republican	September 20, 1881
22	Grover Cleveland	Democrat	March 4, 1885
23	Benjamin Harrison	Republican	March 4, 1889
24	Grover Cleveland	Democrat	March 4, 1893
25	William McKinley	Republican	March 4, 1897
26	Theodore Roosevelt	Republican	September 14, 1901
27	William Taft	Republican	March 4, 1909
28	Woodrow Wilson	Democrat	March 4, 1913
29	Warren G. Harding	Republican	March 4, 1921
30	Calvin Coolidge	Republican	August 3, 1923
31	Herbert Hoover	Republican	March 4, 1929
32	Franklin D. Roosevelt	Democrat	March 4, 1933
33	Harry S. Truman	Democrat	April 12, 1945
34	Dwight D. Eisenhower	Republican	January 20, 1953
35	John F. Kennedy	Democrat	January 20, 1961

LEFT OFFICE	TERMS SERVED	VICE PRESIDENT
September 19, 1881	Died During First Term	Chester Arthur
March 4, 1885	Completed Garfield's Term	Office Vacant
March 4, 1889	One	Thomas A. Hendricks
March 4, 1893	One	Levi P. Morton
March 4, 1897	One	Adlai E. Stevenson
September 14, 1901	Served One Term, Died During Second Term	Garret A. Hobart, Theodore Roosevelt
March 4, 1909	Completed McKinley's Second Term, Served One Term	Office Vacant, Charles Fairbanks
March 4, 1913	One	James S. Sherman
March 4, 1921	Two	Thomas R. Marshall
August 2, 1923	Died During First Term	Calvin Coolidge
March 4, 1929	Completed Harding's Term, Served One Term	Office Vacant, Charles Dawes
March 4, 1933	One	Charles Curtis
April 12, 1945	Served Three Terms, Died During Fourth Term	John Nance Garner, Henry A. Wallace, Harry S. Truman
January 20, 1953	Completed Roosevelt's Fourth Term, Served One Term	Office Vacant, Alben Barkley
January 20, 1961	Two	Richard Nixon
November 22, 1963	Died During First Term	Lyndon B. Johnson

	PRESIDENT	PARTY	TOOK OFFICE
36	Lyndon B. Johnson	Democrat	November 22, 1963
37	Richard Nixon	Republican	January 20, 1969
38	Gerald Ford	Republican	August 9, 1974
39	Jimmy Carter	Democrat	January 20, 1977
40	Ronald Reagan	Republican	January 20, 1981
41	George H.W. Bush	Republican	January 20, 1989
42	Bill Clinton	Democrat	January 20, 1993
43	George W. Bush	Republican	January 20, 2001
44	Barack Obama	Democrat	January 20, 2009
45	Donald Trump	Republican	January 20, 2017

Barack Obama

★ PRESIDENTS MATH GAME ★

Have fun with this presidents math game! First, study the list above and memorize each president's name and number. Then, use math to figure out which president completes each equation below.

1. Woodrow Wilson − Millard Fillmore = ?

2. Millard Fillmore + Rutherford B. Hayes = ?

3. Barack Obama − Millard Fillmore = ?

Answers: **1. James Buchanan** (28 − 13 = 15) **2. Franklin D. Roosevelt** (13 + 19 = 32) **3. Herbert Hoover** (44 − 13 = 31)

LEFT OFFICE	TERMS SERVED	VICE PRESIDENT
January 20, 1969	Completed Kennedy's Term, Served One Term	Office Vacant, Hubert H. Humphrey
August 9, 1974	Completed First Term, Resigned During Second Term	Spiro T. Agnew, Gerald Ford
January 20, 1977	Completed Nixon's Second Term	Nelson A. Rockefeller
January 20, 1981	One	Walter Mondale
January 20, 1989	Two	George H.W. Bush
January 20, 1993	One	Dan Quayle
January 20, 2001	Two	Al Gore
January 20, 2009	Two	Dick Cheney
January 20, 2017	Two	Joe Biden
		Mike Pence

★ WRITE TO THE PRESIDENT ★

You may write to the president at:

**The White House
1600 Pennsylvania Avenue NW
Washington, DC 20500**

You may email the president at:

www.whitehouse.gov/contact

★ GLOSSARY ★

apprentice—a person who learns a trade or a craft from a skilled worker.

cabinet—a group of advisers chosen by the president to lead government departments.

chancellor—a university president.

civil war—a war between groups in the same country. The United States of America and the Confederate States of America fought a civil war from 1861 to 1865.

debate—a contest in which two sides argue for or against something.

debt—something owed to someone, usually money.

Democrat—a member of the Democratic political party. When Millard Fillmore was president, Democrats supported farmers and landowners.

economy—the way a nation uses its money, goods, and natural resources.

Free-Soil—a political party that had power between 1848 and 1854. Its members opposed the extension of slavery into US territories and the admission of slave states into the Union.

immigration—entry into another country to live. A person who immigrates is called an immigrant.

pneumonia (nu-MOH-nyuh)—a disease that affects the lungs and may cause fever, coughing, or difficulty breathing.

Republican—a member of the Republican political party. When Millard Fillmore was president, Republicans supported business and strong government.

running mate—a candidate running for a lower-rank position on an election ticket, especially the candidate for vice president.

stroke—a sudden loss of consciousness, sensation, and voluntary motion. This attack of paralysis is caused by a rupture to a blood vessel of the brain, often caused by a blood clot.

telegraph—a device that uses electricity to send coded messages over wires.

Whig—a member of the Whig political party that was very strong in the early 1800s but ended in the 1850s. Whigs supported laws that helped business.

ONLINE RESOURCES

Booklinks
NONFICTION NETWORK
FREE! ONLINE NONFICTION RESOURCES

To learn more about Millard Fillmore, please visit **abdobooklinks.com** or scan this QR code. These links are routinely monitored and updated to provide the most current information available.

★ INDEX ★